It Happened to Me!
It Will Happen to You!
If You Keep Breathing?

A Chronology of
Life's Events

Dedication
Timothy D. Hartge, (Candidate) Ed.D.

A close personal friend of over 37 years, married for 41 years, father of three, a certified race car driver, a licensed aircraft mechanic, an experienced advertising sales executive, a writer, an avid car enthusiast, a classic auto show organizer, as well as, a professor of Marketing at a Big Ten university. Tim has been a consistent supporter of this author's writing efforts.

His Best Personal Quote:
Wm. F. Buckley, Jr.'s quotation of "if you can't write, you can't think" describes Tim's personal philosophy.

Foreword

In my 35-year career as an executive recruiter, I interviewed thousands of people during which I observed a natural cycle of events, which occurred in everyone's career from the inexperienced to the most highly experienced professional.

With that cycle in mind, I chose to chronologically chart (Back Cover) those events, as YOU will experience them during your life. I called the chart the "Chronology of Common American Life Events."
This reference book is a simple explanation of those events. The book is **not** all-inclusive of everything that will happen; rather it is a consolidation of specific happenings.

Time itself is continuously moving forward never backward and it will never stop. Time affects every aspect of our lives, which influences all of our decisions.

During your life you will experience several interruptions and changes, each will influence the decisions you will make regarding life, employment, and career.

Some people will stay in their chosen career and even with their first employer for their entire work life. Others will change employers and even their careers sporadically, while still others will change both multiple times.

Years ago, it was reported on NBC News that during our work lives people will change:

Jobs: **nine** times
No one deliberately plans to change jobs multiple times, however over a 40-year work life personal opinions change, economic events occur, and undesirable circumstances happen, which may result in you changing jobs.

Careers: **five** times
Correspondingly a person may change their career several times during their life. Many professionals, doctors, lawyers, accountants, engineers, and even teachers decide after a period of time to change their career for many individual reasons. It may be a modification, but it is still a career change. Some changes are drastic in order to course correct for their lifestyle purposes or personal development.

Changing jobs or careers multiple times are **not** recommended, but on occasion it is necessary due to select events and circumstances. Job stability is a good thing.

Charted Contents
(Back Cover)

Period One
Age 18 to 23 years

Now, it Starts!

A pivotal period in your life begins. For possibly the first time you will be making decisions as to how you elect to spend the next few years.

Along with being **Able to Vote,** other alternative choices are plentiful. Do you press ahead with higher education such as college, trade school, join the military, or just get a job to work while making decisions that will impact your future?

Some decisions are Good! Some are Bad!
Society deems some as Good, others as Bad!
Some decisions are Easy, others are Not!

These matters are difficult and frustrating points to ponder. Should you have parents, guardians, and/or close friends, who wish to be involved and to act as "sounding boards" or advisors you are fortunate. In any event you will make the decisions.
It's your life!

Personal **Story**:

After graduation from a mid-west, parochial high school, where I undertook a college preparatory course of study, I enrolled in the university of my choice. College was a different environment. Now, I made the course selections. Now, I selected my schedule according to the course availability and mine. Now, I paid the tuition. Now, I chose whether to go to classes or not. Now, I was responsible for my decisions and my actions. And I got what I deserved both: Good and Bad.

After changing my study curriculum three times and submitting to career psychological testing, I discovered my initial career inclinations were correct. But, after two years, I lost my scholastic edge (GPA) due to too much freedom and was asked to leave the university. It was a wake up call!

This was the era of the Vietnam conflict and the military draft was in force, and it was nothing to fool around with. I did and I lost my draft deferment.

My Father's Proclamation:

Throughout my teenage years my father always said, "If you chose not to go to college you need to have a trade." Since I planned to go to college, I really did not considered any specific trade. So, when I was college-free and through some unusual efforts, I secured a 6-year printing apprenticeship. However, the U.S. government had other ideas for me and sent me their traditional "Greetings" telegram inviting me to spend sometime in the service to my country.

After studying my options, I elected to enlist in the military in order to have some choice of duty preference. Some aspects of the military quickly did not appeal to me, yet others did. During those three years, I came to understand the derivation of the acronym GI, which means I was Government Issue (property).

Following my discharge my attitude was better focused to seek employment and to reengage the furtherance of my education, which I finalized a few years later. Those years spent in the military were crucial in my personal development.

Everyone's life is not predetermined or predestined. It can and will be altered. The decisions you make one day can and will impact other aspects of your life for years in the future.

Note: It wasn't until I was 30 years of age that I discovered the key to life is **<u>Service to Others</u>**!

Period Two
Age 23 to 30 years

Graduation from a **university** while completing a select curriculum allows one to enter his or her 1st professional **Career** and/or **Job.**

At the bare minimum you have publicly proven that you can satisfactorily learn any employer's basic requirements. It is during these early years when employers start "keeping score." They do not utilize any specific grading system; rather they actually observe how you will incorporate all of what you have learned and how you will utilize that knowledge to accomplish the varied tasks for which you were hired. This is how references are developed.

Marriage, Family & Insurance Issues:

The likelihood of **Marriage** becomes increasingly probable. Today, almost all marriage relationships operate in a dual career environment. Once children are added to the marriage further decisions are required. This is the beginning of **Family Issues**. Adequate health **insurance** for the entire family is required. Soon thoughts of further protection in areas of life, disability income, and long-term care (LTC) are also pursued.

Time management becomes critical. Juggling daily schedules involving day-care, baby-sitting, schooling, organized sports, and scholastic events, not to mention other melded family activities, which will become a perpetual consideration.

Graduate School:

As you focus on your career with limited or no real experience, the importance of **graduate school** becomes readily apparent in order to further specialize and/or to expand your knowledge. Graduate school can be accomplished as a fulltime student, night school and/or with online courses.

Job and/or Career changes:

After 4-5 years in the **1st Job** many people feel under utilized, under compensated, even under fulfilled which may cause them to look outside their current employment for greater opportunity. Some call this employment phase as "looking for greener pastures," but remember, the grass may look greener, but it still needs to be mowed.

It is very important for anyone to research and gather information on any new Company, Job and/or Career change before making a change. Circumstances, which cause people to look elsewhere, very well can exist in the new job. If the research is not thoroughly performed employment dissatisfaction may, again, result. Where soon after the common thought is to change jobs again, simply because little time has been invested in this **2nd Job**, therefore a change to a **3rd Job** is easily rationalized. The major problem here is, a person can be labeled a "job jumper." Not a good thing.

A good principle to live by is not to make any decision too quickly without sleeping on it for at least a night. Everything looks different in the morning.

Personal **Story**:

In my late twenties, I was employed as a financial analyst at Chrysler Corporation advancing to four different management positions in six years. Then, the country experienced a severe recession, which affected the corporation, as well as, my employment. I, along with thousands of others, experienced an indefinite layoff.

During my layoff off, a perceived opportunity did present itself to me with a small private employer in the medical sales area. I did the appropriate research on the company including making several "ride along sales calls." The technology of the equipment was something I understood; however my sales aptitude or lack thereof was the challenge.

I did resign my financial position, because of the cyclical nature of the auto industry. Then started my new job and career in the medical sales field.

However, it was when I approached the copy machine that I realized that I had made a huge mistake. The copier wasn't powered up. I had to wait a few minutes for it to "warm up." I was used to copiers running 24/7. The aspect of limited versus unlimited resources from one company to another proved to me that I made a critical career error. The company was way to small to assist me in my development and eventual success.

Remember if you can get hired quickly, you can get fired just as quick. If the opportunity is worthwhile it will be there in a day, two, or even three days later.

Period Three
Age 31 to 40 years

Family Issues:
Many family uncertainties will steadily become more important: children, housing, insurance, geographical relocation, dual career considerations, and possibly even your aging parents will have an impact on your decision-making. Each is financially driven.

Insurance Benefit Issues:
Health Care - Life – Disability - LTC Insurance

It is different for everyone, around the ages of 30-40; people realize the importance of employer provided benefits. People start to understand that any insurance benefit is part of their compensation.

Protection of your health is of paramount concern. The lack of **medical insurance** can result in extreme financial distress. Cost is based upon a person's age, the younger a person is the cheaper the insurance, correspondingly, the older the person is the greater the premium. As of this writing the "law of the land" is universal medical coverage for all.

Life and disability insurance also provide a degree of security to the family. Long Term Care Insurance (LTC) should be considered. It is not only for the senior citizens amongst us. Besides it is cheaper when you are younger. Even if you elect to be self-employed these insurance products will still be required except the expenses of them are to be borne by you.

15

Graduate School:

Naturally, other facets of your life will carry on such as Graduate School. The need for graduate studies may even become a family priority for you to succeed. Your studies may prove to be another hurdle involving school in the evening or online classes. This can be a very stressful period.

Retirement Issues:

Not to be "glossed over" is your eventual Retirement. It is never too early to plan and start saving for this eventuality. I can **guarantee** that if you keep breathing you will get older and older and one day you will desire to retire from your everyday job or career activity.

Around the age of 40, the aspect of your eventual retirement becomes clearer. In order to retire you will need to have sufficient finances set aside to support yourself during this possibly lengthy period. The total amount you will need is sizable and will vary by individual and life style. You will need to research this area like most things in your life. Hiding your money "under a mattress" or in a "piggy bank" will not generate the needed return to attain your goal. A annual goal of 4-8% gain is attainable depending on your propensity for risk and how early you begin. Without some risk you will not attain your goal. Again, the earlier you start investing the better. Regarding retirement savings there are many good books and on-line services available on the subject.

A book I read years ago alerted and educated me to several simple concepts of saving and investing for retirement was "The Power of Money Dynamics" by Venita Van Caspel, CFP. The book got me thinking. To this day, I still regularly use several of the ideas it expressed.

Some people follow the 80-10-10% rule of finance: Live on 80%, Give 10%, and Save 10%.

If your employer allows participation in their retirement program you should participate in the program whether or not your employer contributes anything. You'll be better prepared for tomorrow if you take an active role in your financial well being today.

Also, entrusting someone to manage your funds is an option, however President Ronald Reagan's favorite quote applies here "Trust, but Verify." Do not totally trust anyone with your finances without knowing exactly what they are doing with them.

Self-Employment:
On average this mid-life period (35-40) is also when the inclination towards Self-Employment surfaces and even straddles itself into the next phase of your work life. It may become more of a "now or never" concern. This new employment endeavor commonly results in an entrance to a very different work arena. It can be anything from the industrial market to the restaurant industry or maybe to the financial area. This could be your **3rd** or **4th Job Change** and/or **2nd** or **3rd Career Change**.

Remember, when you are self-employed your success is conditional upon any number of factors: e.g. finances, marketing, the product/service, and the business promotion. Everything associated with your business or service is totally your responsibility.

Hard work is a requirement, but it may not be enough in the end. Then, again, self-employment does workout. In any event, this is when your education coupled with your work experience really comes into focus.

Often after a few years of self-employment, a person seeks the synergy of likeminded professionals. The option of being able to just "bounce" ideas or share decisions with someone else is inviting. In attempting to resolve this longing the end result may be a change back into the employment ranks as an employee. Another change!

Employment Issues:

True Story:
A candidate I interviewed was a president for a national homebuilder who desired to find a new position. He was a proactive manger who interfaced with everyone in the company from the warehouse, to the loading docks, as well as, at the job sites. His reason for making a job change was that he missed talking with people who had broader ideas and opinions other than their pickup trucks, hunting blinds, and the happenings at the local bar. He wasn't a snob; he was a professional whose job lacked the synergy of likeminded professionals in his work life.

: At any time you may experience a period(s) of unemployment. This could be the result of local and/or national economic conditions, which are well beyond your control, or maybe an illness or injury.

Overall, this 10-year period is when your life separates you from your youth into adulthood.

Generation GAP:

So as not to "pour ice water" on your ambitions and/or plans, but as you approach your 40th year you may begin to experience the beginnings of a Generation GAP with your younger co-workers. They unintentionally begin to exclude you from various activities or if you have employees it becomes difficult for you to relate to them. As time moves forward, the more the GAP widens.

You will begin to identify better with the older workers. However, they will also have their own agendas depending where they are in their own Life's Chronology. The first references of you being "Over the Hill" may begin to concern you.

Period Four
Age 41 to 50 years

Employment Issues:

A person works for approximately 40 years, which will include intervals of prosperity and austerity. Accepting a new job or promotion is always exhilarating. Losing a job or getting demoted is always upsetting. In life there are no sure things except for 24 hours in a day, 30 days in a month, and 12 months in a year, meanwhile nothing in life is accomplished without Time and Pressure.

During this ten-year period it is possible that a **5th & 6th Job Change** and even a **4th Career Change** may happen for diverse reasons. Be advised, when you are beset with a seemingly good opportunity it does not mean that you have to accept it. There is something to be said for steadiness in any job or profession.

Retirement Issues:

Time steadily advances at the same pace it did the day before, but it seems to go faster, primarily because you have added more activities to your daily life. One vital activity to be maintained is your regular retirement investing in your future.

Self-Employment:

You are now middle age, better grounded, and financially successful. The likelihood that you will revert back to a role as an employee is unlikely, but still possible.

Generational GAP keeps widening between you and your younger co-workers.

Family Issues:

Twenty-five years have passed since your graduation from college. Your children have matured and are now making their own decisions regarding e.g. college, trade school, military, or employment. These are the same decisions that you were confronted with years earlier. Now, they are your children's concerns. The difference is that your position is to provide advice and maybe even financial assistance.

Health Issues:

Your own health may come more into focus. Some say health issues are genealogical, while others say they are not. Annual physicals, periodic checkups, and exercise become increasingly necessary.

Personal Story:

When I was 46 years old, our secretary walked into my office and said that I should get my blood pressure checked. Now, I felt fine, but the wisdom of the moment was to get it checked. Not having a family doctor, I started dialing the phone for references of doctors. I called one doctor only to find out he only did heart transplants. Didn't need him. Later, I found a doctor through a friend, he didn't have a family doctor either, but he did send his daughter to him. She had a good experience. I called him, spoke with him about my blood pressure, later that afternoon I had a complete physical. I was fine. The good thing was now I had a family doctor. I, now, have ten (10) doctors. Things change after 50 years of age.

Often early during this period the matters of life, disability income, and LTC need to be "tweaked" (updated) for your ever changing lifestyle and family issues.

Period Five
Age 51 to 60 years

Career Changes:

By the age of 55 the last of your career changes should have been made, anyway should you make a career change they are really no longer relevant. You have probably broadened your career explanation to being in a specific industry or profession e.g. Sales, Medicine, or even Finance.

Employment Issues:

Career changes may have stopped, however that doesn't mean that job changes have. Employment reasons may, again, result in a **7th or 8th Job Change**.

Family Issues:

Numerous events can take place in this period such as your children's graduations, engagements, weddings, births, and even deaths. The life cycle repeats itself, again.

Health Issues:

Our daily life encompasses many goals and objectives, but one facet that is not planned for is a serious illness. Simple body chills or a change in seasonal temperatures can bring on a cold or flu and can influence our daily performance. More severe illnesses can have an even greater impact on one's work life. Some times an illness or the results of an accident can last for a day or two, or a week, or even longer, which can have a major effect on one's career. This is why disability income insurance should be considered.

Health Care - Life – Disability - LTC Insurance

Health:

The importance of this item cannot be over stated, because it can be used and needed anytime.

Life:

If your employer provides a Life Insurance benefit be sure to take advantage of it and maximize it as well. If you have to pay for your own Life Insurance typically a Term product is less expensive option.

Disability:

The statistics are one in five (20%) will be able to utilize this insurance, if they have it.

True Story:

In our small executive search company of ten people, we had two individuals that used this disability benefit our company provided.

LTC Insurance:

Securing LTC becomes more realistic for some people. Others may wait, while still others don't believe they will ever use it. They believe their family will care for them if needed. That might be true, however can one really depend on their kids to do that? Their lives may be 50 miles, several hundred miles, even a continent away. Better rethink that one, again.

Retirement Issues:

Increased systematic regular investing is vital along with consistent monitoring of your portfolio performance.

Period Six
Age 61 to 66 years

Generational Issues:

Generational differences continue to separate groups of people. Your concern to fit in with others at this age is minimal. You are now more mature and willing to accept others for themselves. Time changes people and in this instance it is usually for the good.

Health Issues:

Improvement of one's health is our constant daily pursuit. As is often stated, "we are our parents," so therefore genealogic health issues can surface. Every year it seems there are new medical discoveries that will forecast our possible future health issues.

Retirement Issues:

Soon the funds you have regularly invested in for years may be requested by you to support you in retirement. You will continue to monitor performance and may even add to your portfolio.

Family Issues:

A number of factors come into play at this age: Marriage of your own kids, possibly becoming grandparent, your own health, as well as, that of your spouse and your own aging parents.

Travel Opportunities:

Travel is something you may or may not choose to do. Whether it is local, national, or international travel it is expensive. Sufficient savings will be required.

One unpleasant task everyone has before they pass away from this earth is to do some final planning in addition to their interment directions. The minimum requirement anyone should have is a Will. It directs a spouse, family member, a friend, or court authority as to what your final wishes are as to the disposition of your personal finances, assets, and body. Should you accumulate a sizable estate comprised of physical and financial properties you may need more legal direction, such as a Trust. A Trust is to insure that your final wishes are followed, so that your spouse, dependents, charities, etc. receive what you wish.

It is simple – You can't take it with you.

True Story:
A relative of mine was financially successful in his life. Blessed with good health until the age of 90, when he was diagnosed with pancreatic cancer. He immediately thought to secure legal services and to develop a family trust to provide for his wife and extended family. It was completed. He died three weeks later.

A few years later his wife passed away. Problems began immediately. The Trust was never signed, dated, or notarized. His sizable estate then had to be probated. The court did appointed lawyers and accountants who were paid their fees to organize the estate. A year & half later, the probated trust was finalized. The lack of signatures, dates, and notarization caused this needless action.

2nd True Story:

Another close friend of mine accumulated a sizable estate 30 times greater than his ending salary. He saved, but had the problem of looking into the "abyss of death" and planning. It was only after a severe heart attack did he finally get motivated to establish a trust. It was complicated and extensive. Now, that it is done, he is happy, content, and playing golf. He is comfortable knowing that his executor will deal appropriately regarding his final arrangements. And, he still believes the **Detroit** *Lions* will win the Super Bowl - this Year!

Period Seven
Age 66 to 75

Retirement Issues:
Depending on age restrictions a person can apply for their Social Security entitlement, as well as, withdraw funds from a variety of financial investment products in their retirement portfolio to develop their own retirement income.

Truthful Retiree Statements:
"I don't know when I ever had time to work . . .
Retirement is great; I do what I want to do . . .
Life has never been better . . .

Retirement is not as advertised . . .
Too much time on my hands, I am going crazy . . .
All renovation projects eventually come to an end.

Every day is a Saturday . . .
I wish I had saved more . . .
Too much time, too little money . . ."

Generational Issues:
True Story:
A friend took advantage of an early retirement package offered by his employer. As he approached the date of retirement he had a change of heart. But, once he started the process he couldn't stop it.

After two years, he received a call from his old boss asking him if he would like to return to work as a contract employee. He did return and was greeted by his former co-workers with the statement "why?"

It was uncomfortable for a time, approximately three years later; he decided to retire, again.

The lesson here is that sometimes you cannot go back.

Memoirs, Writings & Hobbies:

Not everyone desires to write, but those who can should. I do it for family, friends, and myself. Sometimes, I try to make my writings available to students and others. It is good exercise for my mind.

Estate Issues:

It is always good to review a Will and/or Trust every ten (10) years due to tax law changes, change of beneficiaries, update for any key deaths, as well as, any additions or deletions impacting the Trust.

Interment Issues:

Given life expectancy today is 84 years of age for a non-smoking male most people choose not to think about their funeral and interment expenses. They may feel it is just not in their "budget" other items such as food, housing, tuition, retirement, insurance, and other expenses take precedence. So we think!

The reality of life is that we are only one breath away from our death. It can happen any time, as the result of any number of health related illnesses and/or from accidental injury.

In any event it happens, therefore we have a choice to make plans for our final arrangements or let someone else make them. You have been in charge of such things for years; the responsibility for this event should not be left to anyone else. It's your choice.

Personal Real Story:

Being a veteran of the US Army, I earned the privilege of being buried alongside my fellow servicemen. The peaceful and pristine setting at the Great Lakes National Veteran Cemetery in Holly, Michigan will be my, as well as my wife's, final resting place. I even get to write my own headstone inscription:

"He didn't work well with crowds or committees."

Travel Opportunities:

Often this is a time when you may be able to take advantage of travel opportunities for which you couldn't before retirement. Now, time may be "wide open" permitting you go almost anywhere, anytime, yet travel does involve funds that you may or may not have. Again, you must plan for these occurrences.

Health Issues:

Over this 10-year period old afflictions persist and new afflictions present themselves causing you new frustrations. Doctor visits become commonplace.

9th Post-Retirement Jobs:

For a variety reasons after people retire they have the feeling that they still have more to offer. Renovating a room in the house, playing golf, gardening, or many other retirement activities may not satisfy that feeling. Many seek out some type of work, which does satisfy. One thing is for certain the new job probably will not be in your previous profession.

Volunteering:

One's time is more valuable than money. It sends a message that you care. Not only does another person or group benefit from the assistance, but you also get a very positive lift in your spirit. Even a small amount of time is good.

Period Eight
Age 75 & Beyond

Travel Opportunities:

Depending on your finances and physical stamina you may have the time and freedom to visit areas of the country and the world.

Retirement Issues:

At this age a conservative return of 4% to any *"Nest Egg"* portfolio is recommended in order to make it last.

Volunteering:

Everything here depends on an individual's personal stamina. Some jobs require physical exertion; others can be administrative.

Health & LTC Issues:

Many times as we age serious health conditions do develop which require daily attentive health care, which cannot be rendered by family. If you are fortunate to have planned and secured LTC insurance for this event earlier in life the overall financial impact will be minimized.

Estate Issues:

Plan to have Durable Power of Attorney, Medical Patient Advocate statement, Last Will and Testament, possibly your Trust, Trustee(s) letters, and Final Arrangement instructions, credit card cancellation letters with postage, as well as, other significant letters secured in a location known to your Trustee.

The matter of "eternal rest" is ever present. In time the experience of death does happen to everyone. Most people do not wish to discuss and/or plan for their own funeral or interment expenses. They prefer to leave those decisions to someone else. Simply deferring those decisions to someone else is not being responsible to those you have cared about for years.

It's should be your choice.

Period Nine
Other Issues

Other lifetime experiences many such as:
Unemployment - Relocation - Housing
Injury - Legal - Economic

Unemployment:

Possibly through no fault of yours a lengthy period of unemployment may happen anytime and more than once. It is good to have some savings allocated specifically for this event. It is difficult to make one's career recession proof, even those careers which are favored, usually must make adjustments due to the economy.

Relocation & Housing:

Job and career opportunities may present themselves locally, but in many cases they will involve a geographical relocation of the family. Even a change of personal residence can be considered either a positive or negative event in your life.

Injury & Legal:

Injury to yourself, to someone else, or a property can result in utilization or interface with legal authorities.

In the end there are countless events, which will influence and economically impact a life.

Period Ten
Keep this Book!

Consider this book as a forewarning, an advance notice, a flag, or a Head's Up!

There are items, which you have kept for years e.g. HS class yearbook, college class ring, and still other items for which you worked hard to attain. There will be other new items that you will wish to keep. This book should be one of them.

You may not appreciate the topics discussed herein today, but you **will** later. In the future you **will** need a "spark" for any number of reasons; this book may provide you that spark. The simple knowledge that others have experienced what you are now experiencing should give you a degree of comfort.

www.ingramcontent.com/pod-product-compliance
Lightning Source LLC
Chambersburg PA
CBHW060346290526
45791CB00004B/1560